THIS BOOK BELONGS TO

....

....

....

....

FOR TINA - H.B.
FOR MY FAMILY AND FRIENDS - R.D.

Mantra Lingua Ltd
Global House, 303 Ballards Lane, London N12 8NP
www.mantralingua.com

First Published in 2002 by Mantra Lingua Ltd
Text copyright © Henriette Barkow
Illustration copyright © 2002 Roland Dry
Dual Language Text copyright © 2002 Mantra Lingua Ltd
Audio copyright © 2009 Mantra Lingua Ltd
This sound enabled edition published 2012

Der Rattenfänger

The Pied Piper

retold by Henriette Barkow
illustrated by Roland Dry

German translation by Nick Barkow

MANTRA LINGUA

Manche Leute halten diese Geschichte für wahr, andere nicht. So oder so, will ich euch diese Geschichte erzählen.

Vor uralten Zeiten gab es eine Stadt namens Hameln. Es war eine ganz gewöhnliche Stadt mit ganz gewöhnlichen Leuten, Leuten wie du und ich.

Eines Jahres fielen Ratten in die Stadt ein. Grosse Ratten, kleine Ratten, dicke Ratten, dünne Ratten. Wo man hinschaute, nichts als Ratten!

Some people believe this story is true, and others that it is not. But either way this story I will tell to you.

Many years ago, in the days of old, there was a town called Hamelin. It was an ordinary town, with ordinary people just like you and me.

One year the town had an invasion of RATS. There were big rats and small rats, fat rats and thin rats. Wherever you looked there were RATS!

Man kann sich gut vorstellen, dass die Bewohner der Stadt in helle Aufregung gerieten. Sie stürmten das Rathaus und verlangten vom Bürgermeister sofort was zu unternehmen.

"Was soll ich denn tun?" rief der. "Ich bin schliesslich kein Rattenfänger!"

As you can imagine, the people of the town were very upset. They stormed to the town hall and demanded that the mayor do something.

"What do you expect me to do?" he shouted. "I'm not a rat catcher!"

In diesem Augenblick kam ein Fremder daher. Er war seltsam gekleidet. In der Hand trug er eine Flöte. Die Menge starrte den Fremden an, so, wie man gewöhnlich Fremde anstarrt. Aber dass belästigte ihn nicht.

At that very moment a stranger appeared, wearing the most unusual clothes and holding a pipe in his hand. The crowd stared at the stranger, the way that people often stare at strangers, but that didn't bother him.

Der Fremde ging sofort zum Bürgermeister und stellte sich vor: "Man nennt mich den Rattenfänger. Wenn Sie mir zwanzig Goldstücke zahlen werde ich all diese Ratten wegschaffen."

Das klang wie Musik in den Ohren des Bürgermeisters. "Wenn dir gelingt, was du da sagt, dann werde ich überglücklich sein dich zu bezahlen," rief er.

The stranger walked straight up to the mayor and introduced himself. "They call me the Pied Piper and if you pay me twenty pieces of gold I will take all your rats away."
Well this was music to the mayor's ears. "If you can truly do what you say, I shall be more than happy to pay you," he replied.

Die Bewohner der Stadt standen herum und hörten zu. Dieser sogenannte Rattenfänger, könnte der wirklich alle Ratten verschwinden lassen? Die grossen Ratten und die kleinen Ratten, die jungen Ratten und die alten Ratten?

The town's people waited and watched. Could this so called Pied Piper really get rid of all the rats - the big rats and the small rats, the young rats and the old rats?

Ganz langsam fing der Rattenfänger an auf seiner Flöte zu spielen. Da geschah Unglaubliches. Aus allen Ritzen und Löchern strömten die Ratten auf die Strasse. Wie gebannt von der Musik folgten sie dem Flötenspieler.

The Pied Piper slowly started to play his pipe and an unbelievable thing happened. From every nook and cranny the rats poured out onto the street, and under the spell of the music, they followed the piper.

Sie folgten ihm aus der Stadt Hameln an den Fluss, die Weser. Hier spielte er eine andere Melodie - und mit kläglichem Winseln stürzten sich die Ratten in das eiskalte Wasser, wo sie ertranken.

They followed him out of Hamelin town to the river Weser. Here, the Pied Piper changed his tune and with a mournful wailing, the rats threw themselves into the icy water and drowned.

Der Bürgermeister von Hameln war ein arg geiziger Mensch und fand, warum sollte er einem Fremden irgendwas zahlen. Als der Flötenspieler kam und seine Goldstücke forderte, da lachte der Bürgermeister und schüttelte den Kopf. "Wofür soll ich dir was zahlen, wo doch alle Ratten weg sind?" sagte er.

Now the mayor of Hamelin was a greedy man, and he wasn't going to give any money to a stranger. When the Pied Piper came and demanded his pieces of gold the mayor laughed and shook his head. "Now that the rats are gone why should I give you anything?" he snarled.

Die Leute die herumstanden hörten das. Aber keiner trat für den Flötenspieler ein, obwohl sie doch wussten, dass ihr Bürgermeister im Unrecht war. Sie sagten kein Wort.

The people stood and listened. They didn't stand up for the piper, even though they knew that their mayor was wrong. They didn't say a word.

"Das sollten Sie sich noch einmal überlegen, Bürgermeister," sagte der Flötenspieler. "Wenn Sie nicht zahlen werde ich unvorstellbares Leid über die Stadt bringen."

Schlimmeres als Ratten konnte sich der Bürgermeister nicht vorstellen. Er stapfte davon und rief:
"ICH WERDE DIR NICHTS ZAHLEN - NIEMALS!"

"Think again, mayor!" the piper warned. "If you don't pay, then I will make this town suffer more than you can ever imagine."

Well the mayor couldn't think of anything worse than the rats and so he stomped off shouting:
"I WILL NEVER PAY YOU!"

Am selben Nachmittag, als alle Leute die Schäden an ihrer Stadt beseitigten, stand der Flötenspieler auf dem Marktplatz. Langsam hob er die Flöte an seine Lippen und spielte eine Melodie, die zu beschreiben unmöglich war.

That very afternoon, while the people were busy repairing their town, the Pied Piper stood in the town square. Slowly he lifted the pipe to his lips, and played a tune that no words could describe.

Bei jedem neuen Ton kamen mehr und mehr Kinder,
sie tanzten und sangen zur Musik.

With each new note more and more children appeared,
and danced and sang to the music.

Dann drehte sich der Flötenspieler um und ging zu den Tönen seiner Flöte aus der Stadt hinaus. Ihm folgten alle Kinder gebannt vom Zauber der Musik.

The Pied Piper turned and walked out of the town playing his pipe and all the children followed, caught under the spell of his music.

Die Kinder sangen und tanzten zum Rhythmus der Melodie, so ging es hinauf auf einen Hügel. Dort, am Ende, tat sich ein Tor auf und sie folgten dem Flötenspieler ins Innere - und wurden nicht mehr gesehen. Nur ein Kind blieb, draussen zurück, es konnte nicht so schnell laufen wie die anderen.

Up the hill they danced and sang to the rhythm of the tune. When it looked like they could go no further, a door opened before them. One by one the children followed the Pied Piper into the heart of the hill forever. All except one, who could not keep up with the others.

Als dieser kleine Junge zurückkam in die Stadt, schien es als sei ein Bann gebrochen. Ungläubig starrten die Menschen ihn an, als er berichtete, was geschehen sei. Da weinten sie und riefen nach ihren Kindern - aber sie haben sie nie wieder gesehen.

When the little boy returned to the town it was as if a spell had been broken. The people stared at him in disbelief when he told them what had happened. They called and cried for their children, but they never saw them again.

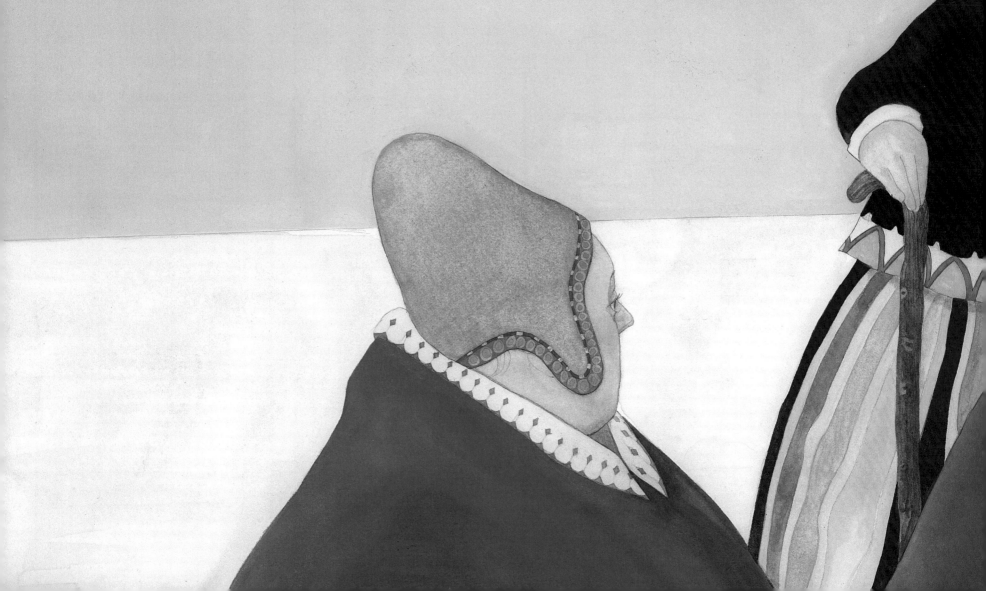

Key Words

town	Stadt
people	Menschen, Leute
rats	Ratten
town hall	Rathaus
mayor	Bürgermeister
rat catcher	Rattenfänger
stranger	Fremder
clothes	Kleidung
pipe	Flöte
crowd	Menge
twenty	zwanzig
pieces of gold	Goldstücke
pied piper	der Rattenfänger

NB known in the German as der
Rattenfänger but the literal translation
is buntegescheckter Flöttenspieler

Schlüsselwörter

music	Musik
playing	spielen
river	Fluss
greedy	geizig
money	Geld
suffer	leiden
children	Kinder
danced	tanzten
sang	sangen
rhythm	Rhythmus
tune	Melodie
hill	Hügel
spell	Zauber, Bann

Die Legende vom Rattenfänger geht zurück auf Begebenheiten, die sich im Jahr 1248 in der deutschen Stadt Hameln ereigneten.

Wer darüber mehr erfahren möchte: Die Stadt Hameln hat eine ausgezeichnete web site in englischer Sprache. http://www.hameln.com/englis

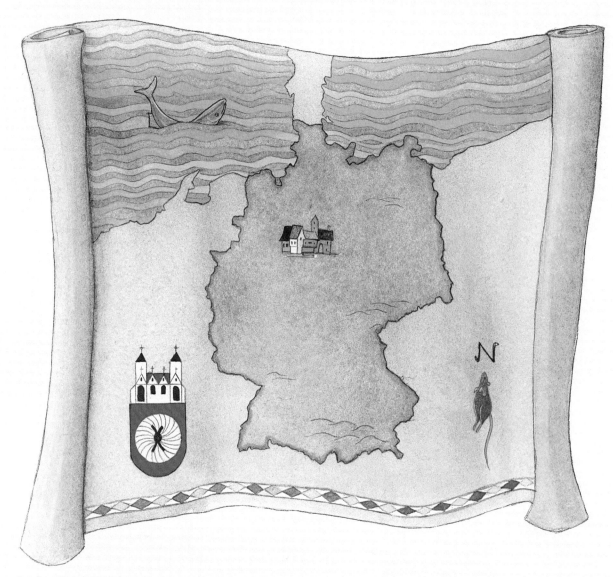

The legend of the Pied Piper originates from events that took place in the town of Hameln in Germany. The story dates back to 1284.

If you would like more information the town of Hameln has an excellent website in English: http://www.hameln.com/englis

If you've enjoyed this bilingual story in German & English look out for other
Mantra titles in German & English

Folk stories in Mantra's World Tales Series

Buskers of Bremen - adapted from the Brothers Grimm
Don't Cry Sly - adapted from Aesop's Fables
Elves and the Shoemaker
The Giant Turnip - a Russian folk story
Goldilocks and the Three Bears
Jill and the Beanstalk - an English folk story
Not Again Red Riding Hood
Three Billy Goats Gruff - a Scandinavian folk story

Mantra's Contemporary Story Series

Alfie's Angels
The Swirling Hijaab
That's My Mum
The Wibbly Wobbly Tooth

Myths and Legends in Mantra's World Heritage Series

Beowulf - an Anglo Saxon Epic
The Children of Lir - a Celtic Myth
Isis and Osiris - an Egyptina legend
Pandora's Box - a Greek Myth

Mantra's Classic Story Series

Walking Through the Jungle
What shall we do with the Boo Hoo Baby?

To see the full range of Mantra's resources do visit our website on www.mantralingua.com